Can Anyone Hear Me?

Can Anyone Hear Me?

Sherry Harris

Can Anyone Hear Me?

Can Anyone Hear Me?
Copyright © 2015 by Fountain of Life Publishers House. All rights reserved.

No part of this publication may be reproduced, stored in a retrieval system or transmitted in any way by any means, electronic, mechanical, photocopy, recording or otherwise without the prior permission of the author except as provided by USA copyright law.

Scripture quotations, unless otherwise indicated, are taken from the *Holy Bible, King James Version*, Cambridge, 1769. Used by permission. All rights reserved.

The opinions expressed by the author are not necessarily those of Fountain of Life Publishers House.

Published by Fountain of Life Publishers House

P. O. Box 922612 Norcross, GA 30010
404-936-3989
Please Email Manuscripts to: publish@pariceparker.biz

Fountain of Life Publishing House is committed to excellence in the publishing industry. The Company reflects the philosophy established by the founder, based on Psalm 68:11, "The Lord gave the word and great was the company of those who published it."

Book design copyright © 2015 by Fountain of Life Publishers House. All rights reserved.
Author: Sherry Harris
Cover Design by Parice Parker
Interior design by Parice C Parker
Editor: Fountain of Life Publisher's House Editor's Team

Published in the United States of America

ISBN: 978-0-9904441-0-7

May 8, 2015

Can Anyone Hear Me?

Can Anyone Hear Me?

Fountain of Life Publishers House

For book orders or wholesale distribution
Website: www.pariceparker.biz

Can Anyone Hear Me?

Can Anyone Hear Me?

TABLE OF CONTENTS
Stories

Introduction 6
1. Follow Suit 7
2. He Doesn't Desire You 8
3. I Got Something To Tell You 12
4. When You Try To Forget 15
5. Sleep Overs 18
6. When Good Samaritans Become Bad 21
7. When Teens Gather 26
8. Be Careful of the Job You Take 28
9. Pray For Wisdom 31
10. Murder Is Not The Answer 35

Sherry Harris

Can Anyone Hear Me?

Introduction

Can Anyone Hear Me is a book that is compiled of astonishing short stories that are actual events that has occurred and will continue. Take heed to these real life events because it could happen to you. I consider them as secrets that has not been told or shared.

Sherry Harris

Can Anyone Hear Me?

STORY ONE

FOLLOW SUIT
"Is this you?"

I was twelve years old and I had to stay the night over someone's house with my sister, only to be violated by someone that I didn't even know! "Why did I let it go that far?" Sometimes if you are someone who has been violated over and over again, it becomes a habit. If you were a child, say around six years old and if something like this happened often in your life, you're not alarmed anymore. You just follow suit. However, it get's very frustrated when no one will listen. Can anyone hear me?

Can Anyone Hear Me?

STORY TWO

HE DOESN'T DESIRE YOU
"Then who?"

"Let this mind be in you which is also in Christ Jesus"

Philippians 2:5

I will never forget one night, I was singing on the balcony of a Resort at about eleven o'clock at night. I was singing about a love that God had shown me in my life and there was no one in comparison. All of a sudden, a woman walked by as I was singing. She walked away from me out towards the water. I must have sung at least one hour and thirty minutes or more. The woman began to walk once again toward me only to look up at me. As I looked upon her, I noticed that she was crying. I went down the stairs to comfort her.

Can Anyone Hear Me?

She was chanting, "I'm tired, I'm tired." I began to say, "God will give you rest. She began to speak. I know that I am not supposed to divorce but He didn't say that I could not separate.

As we began to talk, she said, "I gave my life to be a mother to our two children. My career, I gave up. I was the wife who put on party. I showed hospitality, put on the pretty face and no one even knew how I felt during my marriage of nearly three decades. I am only forty something years old and my husband has not had sex or even looked at me in 10 years. I have been faithful and I don't understand what has happened. I even tried to see if he was having an affair and still couldn't find no evidence. I am a faithful and dedicated wife and mom"

Can Anyone Hear Me?

One thing that I noticed is that we have two children and I look and see that both of our children go to college. When it came to our son, he has to do everything right or face consequences. With our daughter, whatever she wanted, it was done. Whether it was in town or out of town.

They would all meet up there on a very important engagement or everyone who was supposed to be there. He wanted everyone there but her daughter, who had sent a message, that she may not make it. It caused uproar with the husband however it was a must that the daughter was present. In our conversation, I asked, "Would you be able to handle it if the problem or person you were looking for is right among you or your husband. Thy is why your husband no longer having intimacy with you?" "Is it because he is now intimate

Can Anyone Hear Me?

with the daughter instead of you?" "Would you be surprised?" She replied, "No, I would not." We then prayed. While, I was talking to her, I did not notice that she had been drinking but I was so glad that I could be of some help. The devil did not win. I obeyed and God prevailed. "If he does not desire you, then who?"

Can Anyone Hear Me?

STORY THREE

I GOT SOMETHING TO TELL YOU
Girl: Mom, I got something to tell you

Mom: What girl?

Girl: When I come home and you're not here and I have to go out and get our baby brother off of the bus, there is the neighbor. He always be waving at me an smiling

Mom: Ah girl, you know he just wave

Girl: Well mom, he doesn't be looking at me the right way

Mom: You let me know if he tries to touch you or something like that

Girl: Mom, but he don't look at me right.

Can Anyone Hear Me?

Mom: I'll talk about it when I get back home

Girl: Ok mom

Narrator: Tuesday goes by and goes out and get the child. By Thursday, once again, she goes out. She came in the apartment building. The gentleman not only had a smiled at her but at this particular time, he doesn't even have a shirt on.

Girl: Mom, that neighbor keep smiling at me and he is standing in the hallway near the apartment door

Girl: Yeah, but as long as he don't touch you

Girl: But, I don't like the way he smiles at me

Narrator: Two days go by and mom still haven't listened. Shortly after the incident, the young girl

Can Anyone Hear Me?

began to give in to the neighbor. When he waved and smiled, he pursued and she gave in. She tried to tell her mom before it got worst but she did not listen or see the sign. As she grew up to become a woman, one day her mother asked, "When was your first relation and she said, "Mom, remember the neighbor that lived in the apartment building we lived in some years ago? We began to become good friends and he helped me a lot with my little brother. Things happened in the apartment when you were not there. Yes, that is when it happened. I tried to tell you."

Can Anyone Hear Me?

STORY FOUR

WHEN YOU TRY TO FORGET

Imagine being in junior high school and being excited to know you're at another level of education. It's your first time starting junior high but in your home, something happened to stop all of the joy you seem to have. You feel so over burdened by what happened. You don't know how to tell anyone because of what someone might say sooner or later, you have to tell.

Sometimes I slept in the basement on a couch and then someone came to violate me. This person is close to the family. He came in the basement. I could feel someone on me. I soon woke up in a position. The person tells me to be quite. I said a couple of words, "Get up." He still approached me. I was trying to resist but he

Can Anyone Hear Me?

continued, then shortly after-wards I did not come on my menstruation. I got very concerned. "What am I going to do?" I might be hated for what has happened to me.

I did not want to remember how a supposed to be family member crawled on top of me. It was disgusting to me. When I remember I also did not know what to say. I felt lost and ashamed and I was only twelve years old. I started sleeping more, eating more and getting bigger. It was time to tell the secret. This was hard to tell. When I went to the doctor and got the results, I was seven months pregnant. I was ashamed and hurt for what had happened to my life. It was a nightmare and nothing could be done but to go into labor. It was told to my mother that someone did this to your child and you could get them for rape but my mother did not

Can Anyone Hear Me?

know who it was. I did not want her to know who it was.

Shortly after the doctors appointment, we went home. I had to tell my mother what took place in her basement of how he crawled up on me and did his thing. I was so ashamed and could not tell anyone. I tried to forget.

Can Anyone Hear Me?

STORY FIVE

SLEEPOVERS

Every child should know the signs of a good sleep over.

- We are gone to have a sleep over
- All of the children are from seven to ten years old
- The sleep over has games and singing
- Dancing with one another
- Telling stories
- When sleep, it is time to sleep

Every child should know the signs when having a bad sleepover.

- Taking clothes off in front of one another
- One thing leads to another
- Someone wants to get under the cover with you not to sleep
- Touch in the places below yourself

Can Anyone Hear Me?

- It is time to wake up and go to the head of the sleepover

Signs of There is a Problem
Adults in trouble…

- When there is no sexual intimacy with the spouse, this can leave room for committing adulterous and fornicating acts.
- When one has a controlling spirit or behavior out of conduct
- When someone is telling you when to eat or sleep
- Coming and going is totally under submission
- To be seduced in all forms which allowed
- Bondage, prostitution, having sex with other people

Children having problems…

- There are signs when a child has to do everything for another child and it can be their brother or sister

Can Anyone Hear Me?

- Power over the child that is serving the other
- The older child can have destructive behaviors that can make them do sexual things
- Threatening them not to reveal it to anyone

Can Anyone Hear Me?

STORY SIX

WHEN GOOD SAMARITANS BECOME BAD

I know it seems unbelievable that someone you see praising the Lord as though they love the Lord and but know this person is totally different! The person has a twist of faith of becoming evil.

Once upon a time, I met this young woman through a pastor. She was young, beautiful and seemed very friendly. On this day, the pastor of the church was having a revival or special service. I was invited to come by a member of the church. After the service was over, we talked and talked. Shortly after, we went to the pastor's house to rest on that night. It was important for the young lady to take her child to the hospital the

Can Anyone Hear Me?

next morning however the young lady did not have anyone to take her to the appointment. I volunteered to take her to the appointment.

On the journey, she began to talk to me. The young lady told me she had just got out of jail last night and she was picked up by the pastor. Shortly after she told me she was a foster child and that her family lived somewhere near the city. Then, she began to share with me that she has another child. Someone in the pastor's church is taking care of her child. I asked, "How old is the child?" She said he was around three years old. She said that she wanted me to see her other child after we left the hospital. The appointment was over here.

We began our journey back where she lived. She took me to her foster parent's house. I met them. She

Can Anyone Hear Me?

explained to them that I took her to the appointment. She had her baby boy with her. The visit was not long. It was about one hour and a half.

Then we left to go and meet her other child who has been living with the church people. She began to tell me that they were taking care of her child for her. I began to ask why? She explained somehow that it was best for the child. She was able to take care of the child who was about one. He had some challenges that had to be treated and tested so he was with her all the time. The other child was in the care of the church people.

I asked her who was the pastor to her? She said he is someone who always helps her. Throughout our conversation, she let me know she was somewhat troubled in her spirit. I felt so bad knowing that she

Can Anyone Hear Me?

was being treated like this by the pastor. She was having children for or by him. He was making sure that the children got the proper care they needed.

The young lady was nice looking but was special and needed help in so many ways. She told me that she had a stealing problem and she goes to jail a lot. I was with her half the day and then a problem occurred. I was told by the pastor that I needed to go home now! I was at the house with the church people who had the other baby. He said to me, "You need to leave here. Look, you are not going to tear my church apart!" I began to get sad. I didn't know why he was saying this. I noticed that he was pretty upset. I was a threat to him and his church.

Can Anyone Hear Me?

The Deacon checked my car out preparing for me to go back home safely. Shortly after, the Pastor got a call from the Bishop to put me up in the hotel and gave me gas money. He did just that.

That was really frightening to me! I learned that a young innocent lady was being taken advantage of by a man who says that he is a Pastor, just to be used as an object and a human being. We as people in leadership are going to pay for how we miss use with authority. When someone don't understand how you are going to use them and for what purpose and cannot tell you, shame on you! God help your soul. This is what happens when a good Samaritan goes bad.

Can Anyone Hear Me?

STORY SEVEN

WHEN TEENS GATHER

When teens get together, they do many things depending on the crowd they associate with. Some teens don't tell what's really going on among them, in their group and when they are together. I've been told. I raised boys. Most of the time, they choose sports and that means a lot of action with other boys after school.

Some boys share that they touch each other on the butt, leg and chest. This can be their ego. "We want to be the best," is what they say to a sports person. Some said that they even watch some entertainment, which is porn, and some say that they get in the mood to be sexual but there are no women around. This doesn't include all boys but some. All boys do not insist on

Can Anyone Hear Me?

doing these things to each other engaging in sex with one another. Some say, "I won't do it hard," or "If you let me, I'll let you." This is what happens when teens get together.

Can Anyone Hear Me?

STORY EIGHT

BE CAREFUL OF THE JOB YOU TAKE

This could happen to anyone

Be careful of the job that you take. When the deacon says that he has a job, make sure someone knows what type of job that he is asking for you to do. Deacon spoke to one of the young men. "I got a job for you to do." The young man said, "What is it and will I be able to get paid?" The deacon replied, "Meet me at the church at 5:30 pm. The young man was glad that he was going to get a job and get paid only to get to the church to find out about the job that he was getting.

The deacon told him that you won't have to do much, you just let me show you. It required the young man to

Can Anyone Hear Me?

let him go down on him and he would get paid. You should be careful of the job that you take.

Babysitting can be good or bad. On this babysitting job, I thought that I was to sit with two small children. It didn't take long. In fact, it became an overnight job. I was to watch the small children for a short time but the parent decided to come back home early. He wasn't ready but he was supposed to take me home. The time had passed by so fast. The parent replied, "You and the children can sleep in the bed and I'll sleep in the living room but as the night approached, the parent said that the bed was big enough for all of us. He asked if he could get into the bed. The children began to fall asleep and the parent decided to approach the babysitter. He said, "Just let me touch it, it will be ok and I won't hurt

Can Anyone Hear Me?

you." "I'll make sure that you get paid." Be careful of the job you take.

Can Anyone Hear Me?

STORY NINE

PRAY FOR WISDOM
James 1:5
If any of you lack wisdom, let him ask of God that giveth to all man liberally and upbraideth not; and it shall be given him.

This was a very happy time in my life. I had just gotten my children back from being gone for me for five years. The feeling of being without my children was not a good feeling for my life. I became a mother at a very young age. I was only twelve years old when I had my first child. By the age of eighteen years old, I had four children. Something very tragic had happened. It was said that my children were taken away from me for neglect. Back then, I did not have a safe home for my children so they were placed in someone else's home.

Can Anyone Hear Me?

Having babies was pretty much all that I knew. When all of that happened to me, I felt lost. Before that took place, I lost a child through SIDS, Sudden Infant Death Syndrome. I was sixteen. My second daughter was three months old. It was hard but I made it through with the help of God. I thought, now I have to face to loose all of my children?

I was devastated, frightened and felt as though I was loosing my mind to where I ended up in a behavioral center. I was told that I was having anxiety. I felt so alone. I had to start all over by myself. I had to suffer the consequences of what it was like of loosing something very dear to my heart.

Can Anyone Hear Me?

Soon after that, I began to realize that wallowing in my pitty was not going to get my children back home with me. I got myself together and began to learn and achieve the guidelines. I needed to become a responsible mother. I went to parenting classes. I went to social events to listen on how to raise children in a safe environment. I soon accomplished some goals. I got into school, found a little work and managed to get a home for my children. After following the guidelines, they were able to live with me again after five years!

I was so happy only to face another setback. Shortly after, my children returned, things were not going so well. I felt what I suspected could cause me to loose everything again. I worked so hard for me to get my children back! I was not certain but I did not want to be left in the dark so I talked to God and asked for

Can Anyone Hear Me?

wisdom. After a few months went by, I prayed, "Please God, don't let me loose my children again. I really need you." What I believe was going to happen could have really torn me apart. I couldn't tell no one, not even my own mother! My mother had always been very concerned for my children and me. If I told someone about my situation, I could have lost everything so I went back to God for more wisdom.

Some things we do not choose to bare but God knows how much we can bare. God answered all of my prayers and got me out of the fire! I say to every parent raising children, "We must pray for wisdom." I still have my children.

Can Anyone Hear Me?

STORY TEN

MURDER IS NOT THE ANSWER
St. John 10:10
"The thief cometh not, but to steal and to kill, and to destroy: I ma come that they might have life, and that they live it more abundantly"

Living for the Lord is such a blessing. Knowing that you belong to God is awesome! I remember being used by the heavenly father to intervene in someone else's life before something seriously took place. I went to visit my sister in the Lord church. When I was there, I noticed that her child began speaking to her rudely and was out of order, sort of speaking. I prayed that it would not escalate and get out of hand. As the mother and daughter continued talking, I spoke out and said, "I'm going to leave now." I believed that I might need

Can Anyone Hear Me?

to give them some privacy. Once I got up to leave, I said, "I'll get with you later." I went out to my car. I drove out of the driveway of my sister's house and went down the road.

All of a sudden, a small voice said, "Go back and tell her." I kind of said to myself, "Tell her what?" Then the voice came back and said, "Go back to the house." I then began to think. I needed to go back but what will I say to her? I just knew that I was supposed to go back. When I arrived to the house, she answered the door. I entered and said, "I have to tell you something." She

Can Anyone Hear Me?

replied, "What is it?" I then asked for her to sit down so that I could tell her about her daughter's reaction. I began to tell her that she could not protect her daughter. She then replied, "Protect her from what?" I then began to share with her that your daughter is being violated and the violator is your husband, the stepfather! My sister asked, "Who has shared this information with you?" I told her that no one had. I was lead from the spirit to come and let her know what was going on with her daughter. When I was coming back to your house, I did not know what I was going to say. I know that I had to tell you so I obeyed.

My sister shared with me about three years ago in her house, they had to get counseling about it. She replied, "I know that you did not know this." She also said, "I already warned my husband that if I ever catch him

Can Anyone Hear Me?

touching my daughter again that I was going to kill him!" I immediately said, "Murder is not the answer!"

The Lord does not want you to murder anyone and that's why I had to tell you. The Lord comes to give you life that you may have it more abundantly. If you murder someone, you will not even be here for your daughter and you may be locked up for life.

My sister and I began to pray that God would give her guidance as in what to do and how to respond. We believed in God's work on behalf of the family to get though this and to God be the glory! I am so glad that my Lord used me to intervene and let my sister know that murder is not the answer!

Can Anyone Hear Me?

Acknowledgment's

First and most of all To Jesus my Lord and Savior for strength.
My Husband Assistant - Deacon Dennis Harris for supporting me from the beginning to the end.
To all my loving children, grandchildren, and great grands for enduring with me on this journey, especially my dear daughter Veronica.
My Big Brother - Tyrone Hill you encouraged me on how to write.
My Big Sister - Willie Ann Hill Stokes prayed for the completion of my book.
Minister Felicia Hill Moore for believing this book Can Anyone Hear Me will help others.
Joanna Hill thanks for rooting for me - "Auntie - Sherry You Can Do It!"
Minister Philana Reed thanks for never giving giving up on me.
Pastor Nelle Kennedy thanks for letting me know that so many needs to hear this.

Can Anyone Hear Me?

Apostle Parice Parker for seeing the urgency of Can Anyone Hear Me to help others at such a time as this.

Can Anyone Hear Me?

Biography

Pastor Sherry Harris

Like the melodic tunes in music, Pastor Sherry H. Harris has been instrumental in multiple aspects of family, business and the community. Some of her greatest achievements in life start with home. While Mrs. Harris is dedicated to Deacon Dennis Harris

Can Anyone Hear Me?

who she described as a wonderful god fearing man, love is also shared through giving the ultimate support system to their kids and grand daughter to all she assisted in raising. Together, they accomplished to bring up eleven children. Remarkably, nine of them have already graduated! Today, there are only two still left in the nest. She has also been blessed with one great-grandchild. In her eyes, none of this could have been made possible without the endorsement from the higher power in which they serve!The history of her determination has never wavered because Pastor Sherry Harris is a goal-oriented individual. Her Equivalency Diploma was obtained at Itawamba Community College, which is located in the state of Mississippi. Being the CEO of Kingdom of God Helpers pushed her energy in an upward mode to continue her missionary work across the United States.

Can Anyone Hear Me?

Evangelist Harris is also a college student at the golden age of fifty! Business and Psychology are her majors. It is a dream come true because not only does she love to lead by example, her milestones can be imprinted in the memories of others! Amongst sharing personal testimonies, enjoying other hobbies such as writing, sales, helping other families as a whole unit, counseling, mentoring, feeding the homeless and educating others with life skills is what fills her passionate spirit. Other extracurricular activities explored are song writing, reading, and performing arts, visiting parks, learning about different kinds of history and traveling. Sister Strengthen Sisters, Caring Hearts of America, NAPW - National Association Professional Women, and Strathmore's Who's Who are organizations that Pastor Harris is affiliated with. She loves helping other individuals! While Pastor Harris holds many titles including being licensed and ordained, her main

Can Anyone Hear Me?

goal is to see that all individuals know that spreading the word of the gospel is truly the way! For many years, she has followed her calling when the introduction to do so came from Evangelist, Faye Brown of GAM, Grace Apostolic Ministries in Oxford, Mississippi. That opportunity birthed Coming Clean Ministries. She is currently the vice-president of Power Sight Entertainment, located in Richmond, Virginia. Working alongside esteemed artists, Pearline Wood and Dorinda Clark Coles has kept Pastor Harris humbled and now she is passing down her award winning accomplishments and educational experiences to make aspiring believer's just as phenomenal!She is a Chicago, Illinois native, who now resides in Charlotte, North Carolina, Pastor Harris would like to invite you, the reader to connect with her!

Can Anyone Hear Me?

Contact Information for Pastor Sherry Harris

Mailing address:
P. O. Box 241451 Charlotte, North Carolina 28224
www.kogh.net

Can Anyone Hear Me?

www.ingramcontent.com/pod-product-compliance
Lightning Source LLC
Chambersburg PA
CBHW071802040426
42446CB00012B/2670